WHAT MAKES DIFFERENT Sounds?

WHAT MAKES DIFFERENT
Sounds?

By Lawrence F. Lowery

Illustrated by Susan Dolesch

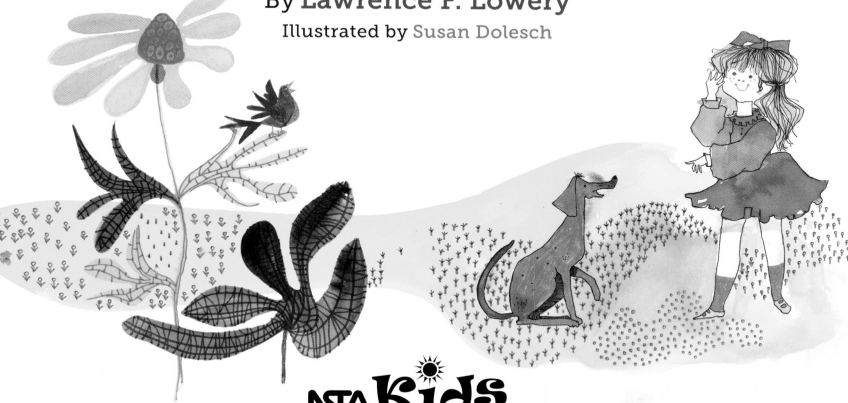

NSTA Kids
National Science Teachers Association
Arlington, Virginia

NSTA Kids
National Science Teachers Association

Claire Reinburg, Director
Jennifer Horak, Managing Editor
Andrew Cooke, Senior Editor
Wendy Rubin, Associate Editor
Agnes Bannigan, Associate Editor
Amy America, Book Acquisitions Coordinator

ART AND DESIGN
Will Thomas Jr., Director
Joseph Butera, Cover, Interior Design
Original illustrations by Susan Dolesch

PRINTING AND PRODUCTION
Catherine Lorrain, Director

NATIONAL SCIENCE TEACHERS ASSOCIATION
Gerald F. Wheeler, Executive Director
David Beacom, Publisher

1840 Wilson Blvd., Arlington, VA 22201
www.nsta.org/store
For customer service inquiries, please call 800-277-5300.

Lexile® measure: 550L

Library of Congress Cataloging-in-Publication Data
Lowery, Lawrence F., author.
  What makes different sounds? / by Lawrence F. Lowery ; illustrated by Susan Dolesch.
    pages cm. -- (I wonder why)
  Audience: K to grade 6
  ISBN 978-1-936959-44-0
  1. Sounds--Juvenile literature. 2. Sound-waves--Juvenile literature. I. Dolesch, Susanne, 1932- illustrator. II. Title.
  QC225.5.L684 2012
  534--dc23
                        2012026550

eISBN 978-1-936959-59-4

Introduction

The *I Wonder Why* books are science books created specifically for young learners who are in their first years of school. The content for each book was chosen to be appropriate for youngsters who are beginning to construct knowledge of the world around them. These youngsters ask questions. They want to know about things. They are more curious than when they are a decade older. Research shows that science is these students' favorite subject when they enter school for the first time.

Science is both *what* we know and *how* we come to know it. What we know is the content knowledge that accumulates over time as scientists continue to explore the universe in which we live. How we come to know science is the set of thinking and reasoning processes humans use to get answers to the questions and inquiries in which we are engaged.

Scientists learn by observing, comparing, and organizing. So do children. These thinking processes are among several inquiry behaviors that enable us to find out about our world and how it works. Observing, comparing, and organizing are fundamental to the more advanced processes of relating, experimenting, and inferring.

The five books in this set of the *I Wonder Why* series focus on inquiry and various content topics: animal behavior, plant growth, physical characteristics of sound, animal adaptations, and mathematical measurement. Inquiry is a natural human attribute initiated by curiosity. When we don't know something about an area of our interest, we try to understand by asking questions and by doing. The five books are titled by questions children may ask: *How Does a Plant Grow? What Can an Animal Do? What Does an Animal Eat?*

What Makes Different Sounds? and *How Tall Was Milton?* Children inquire about plants, animals, and other phenomena. Their curiosity leads them to ask about measurements, the growth of plants, the characteristics of sounds, what animals eat, and how animals behave. The inquiries lead the characters in the books and the reader to discover the need for standard measures, the characteristics of plant growth, sound, and animal adaptations.

Each book uses a different approach to take the reader through simple scientific information from a child's point of view: One book is a narrative, another is expository. One book uses poetry, another presents ideas through a fairy tale. In addition, the illustrations display different artistic styles to help convey information. Some art is fantasy, some realistic. Some art is bright and abstract, some pastel and whimsical. The combining of art, literary techniques, and scientific knowledge brings the content to the reader through several instructional avenues.

In addition, the content in these books correlates to criteria set forth by national standards. Often the content is woven into each book so that its presence is subtle but powerful. The science activities in the Parent/Teacher Handbook section within each book enable students to carry out their own investigations that relate to the content of the book. The materials needed for these activities are easily obtained, and the activities have been tested with youngsters to be sure they are age appropriate.

After students have completed a science activity, rereading or referring back to the book and talking about connections with the activity is a deepening experience that stabilizes the learning as a long-term memory.

Every day after school, twins Jane and Jim walk from their school to their home, passing the familiar busy streets, the calm park, and the empty house. Jane and Jim see the same neighbors, workers, pets, and even the same ice cream man.

But one day …

"Oh!" exclaimed Jane. "That sound scared me."

"WOW. It was loud. I didn't expect it," said Jim. "It scared me, too."

"Look." Jane pointed. "All the people on the street were surprised by the sound. I think they wonder where it came from. They wonder what made the sound."

"I wonder too," Jim said.

Soon Jane and Jim heard the bang again, this time with honking and ringing.

"Listen, Jim," said Jane. "That's another sound! But it didn't scare me."

"The sound is telling us something," replied Jim.

"It's music," said Jane. "The sound tells us there is a band playing music."

"I like the sound of music. Let's go listen!" said Jim.

Jane and Jim followed the sound of drums, horns, and stomping feet right to the town's park. The park was not quiet but instead was full of music.

Jane and Jim had learned about music and sound in school that very day. They had learned that all sounds are made by vibrations. The teacher even used a drum, like the one in the band, to show how vibration causes sound.

"Do you remember that our teacher had a drum and hit the head of it with a drumstick?" asked Jim. "It made a loud sound."

"Yes," said Jane. She remembered how the teacher had put a few grains of salt on the drum and hit it again. The salt had bounced around. "She showed us that the drum head vibrated when it made a sound."

The drum head had moved back and forth very fast, and the air next to it moved quickly too. The sound moved away from the drum and traveled to her ears.

Shhhhhh

In class, Jane and Jim had learned not only about loud sounds and vibrations but also about soft sounds and vibrations.

"Whisper in your partner's ear," their teacher had said.

When Jane had whispered in Jim's ear, her voice sounded soft. It had sounded soft because her voice made the air vibrate gently.

A man in the band was striking an instrument called a triangle. It made a ringing sound.

"That sound reminds me of wind chimes," said Jane.

"The triangle makes a soft ringing sound when it vibrates," added Jim.

Jane and Jim remembered that only vibration can cause sounds. But when something vibrates too slowly, it does not make a sound. When something vibrates too quickly, it also does not make a sound. The triangle vibrated just right for the sound to reach Jane's and Jim's ears.

"The triangle vibrates to make sound! So do the drum and the horn," said Jane. "What else vibrates to make noise?"

GRRRRRR

"Listen to the dog, Jane," said Jim. "The growl is a low sound."

"That sound must be caused by vibration too!" said Jane.

The familiar walk had now become very different. Walking past the park and along the sidewalk, Jane and Jim started to hear many different sounds.

They heard a group of children talking, laughing, whistling, and singing as they played.

A policeman blew a whistle that was loud and shrill. The policeman used the whistle to tell drivers to stop or go. People paid attention to the policeman and his whistle.

"Listen, Jim," said Jane. "That's another loud sound."

"It's a siren," replied Jim. "That sound tells us something."

"It sounds like an ambulance. Maybe it is hurrying to help somebody who is hurt," said Jane.

"Or maybe it is a police car that is in a hurry," suggested Jim.

"Look! It's a fire engine. It's probably going to put out a fire." Jane pointed.

"The fire engine's siren tells everyone to get out of the way," Jim said. "The sound is high and loud."

VRRROOOM

Jane and Jim heard many more loud
sounds along the city street.

Some were loud and unpleasant.

As a worker hammered a hole in the street
and a driver steered his bus around, Jim
covered his ears.

Jane remembered how the vacuum
cleaner at home was a loud sound.

Jane and Jim continued their walk home, nearing the neighbor's empty house.

As a jet flew overhead, Jane covered her ears too.

"It's so loud," she said. "It could hurt your ears if you were near it. I think I like sounds that are usually soft and low. I don't like sounds that are loud," said Jane.

"The jet must make very strong vibrations," said Jim.

RUSTLE

RUSTLE

The sound of the plane eventually faded away.
But the yard was not silent.

Jane and Jim could hear the sound the leaves were making
in the trees. The leaves were making a soft rustling sound.

"How do the leaves make that sound?" said Jane.

RUSTLE

RUSTLE

"The wind must make the leaves' sound," said Jim.
"When the breeze blows through the trees, it moves the
leaves. The leaves rub against each other and vibrate.
The vibrations travel through the air to our ears, and
we hear the leaves rustle."

Jane and Jim reached the old empty house.

"Do you think there are sounds in the empty house?" asked Jim.

"Let's go find out," replied Jane.

The door to the house was open, so they went
inside and listened.

They heard the wood floors creak and crack.
But how could that be? What could be vibrating?

Sounds in an empty house could come
from the house itself.

Sometimes houses vibrate in the morning
when they warm up after a cool night.

Sometimes houses vibrate in the evening
when they cool down after a warm day.

As Jane and Jim listened, they realized that sounds in an empty house could also come from wind. The wind shook the shutters and the windows. These sounds were louder than the rustling leaves.

Jane and Jim then wondered about an empty street or an empty park. The town's streets and the park were empty at night. Would anyone hear noises at night?

"Many animals travel through the park at night," Jim said. "You may not see the animals, but you can hear them if you listen."

Hoooooooo
Hooooooooo

"You can hear croaking frogs, a hooting owl, or chirping katydids. Their sounds tell you that they are there in the dark," Jane said.

Night sounds are usually louder than the sounds in an empty house.

Jim reminded Jane of other night sounds.

la lala

"Mom likes to sing to our baby sister to put her to sleep,"
he said. The songs their mother sings are soft and low.
Jim wondered if the singing was louder than the sounds
in the park at night.

At the end of the walk, Jane and Jim arrived home. Jane saw her next-door neighbors playing under a tree where birds perched on a branch above.

"Do you hear that bird?" she asked. "On our walk today, we learned a lot about sounds. Sounds range from low to high and high to low. Sounds range from very soft to very loud. I know better which sounds I like and which ones I do not like.

And by really listening, we heard many sounds that I usually don't hear, even when the sound is there. I liked listening to so many different sounds ... birds singing, people laughing, leaves rustling, and music playing ... "

What sounds do you like to hear?

WHAT MAKES DIFFERENT *Sounds?*

Parent/Teacher Handbook

Introduction

What Makes Different Sounds? is about twins Jim and Jane and an atypical walk home from school. The walk starts with a loud noise, and they are interested in this new noise, so Jim and Jane continue walking. Along the way, they become interested in the many sounds they hear, including street sounds (e.g., fire engine), night sounds (e.g., a hooting owl), and even sounds in an empty house. They wonder what makes the different sounds. From their observations, they realize that some sounds are helpful and some give them information. They explore high and low sounds, loud and soft sounds, and pleasant and unpleasant sounds.

Inquiry Processes

Observing, comparing, and grouping are inquiry processes that enable the characters in this story to better understand the source and function of some sounds. By adding information they learned in school, the characters realize how sounds are made and transferred to their ears.

Content

All sounds are made when objects vibrate. A vibrating object puts pressure on the molecules in the air around it. Those molecules push on other air molecules and so on, creating a wave that moves away from the source of the vibration. Sound needs a medium to transport a sound wave. It can be a solid, liquid, or gas such as air. Sound cannot be transported in a vacuum.

Sound travels through air (20 °C or 68 °F) at 768 miles or 1,236 kilometers per hour. It travels faster through liquids and some solids.

This book conveys two characteristics of sound vibrations in the simple terms *pitch* (high and low sounds) and *volume* (loudness).

Pitch is the idea that some sounds we hear are high, while other sounds are low. The speed of vibration determines the pitch. A fast vibration produces a higher sound, whereas a slower vibration produces a lower pitch sound.

Volume can be identified by hearing sounds that are loud or soft. Loudness relates to the pressure a vibration produces. The stronger the pressure, the louder the sound.

Science Activities

Seriating Sounds by Pitch

Tap different objects and listen to the pitch each produces. Seriate the objects from the lowest to highest pitch.

Seriating Sounds by Volume

1. Look back at *What Makes Different Sounds?* and identify the objects that make sound. Order the objects from loudest to softest.

2. Collect pictures of machines. Order the pictures by the loudness of the sound each produces.

Making Sound Vibrations Visible

Sound vibrations are usually too rapid to be seen. Try the following activities to observe vibrations:

1. Stretch a rubber band tightly around three nails on a board. Hang several small strips of paper, creased in half, over one section of the band. Pluck the section and observe how the paper strips move. The paper strips can also be placed over the strings of musical instruments and observed when a string is played.

2. If you have a tuning fork, tap the tines and slowly place one into the surface of a glass of water. Note the waves made by the vibrations.

3. Put a small amount of fine sand or salt on a drumhead. Steadily tap the drumhead and watch how its vibrations make the pieces of sand jump around.

Grouping Sounds

Different sounds can be sorted into groupings. Make lists of sounds under the following groupings:

Pleasant Sounds	Unpleasant Sounds
School Sounds	Home Sounds
Outdoor Sounds	Indoor Sounds
Loud Sounds	Soft Sounds
High Sounds	Low Sounds
Sounds People Make	Sounds Animals Make
Morning Sounds	Evening Sounds

Another way to group sounds is to compare sound makers and the types of sounds they produce.